MUSEUM OF ACCIDENTS

Also by Rachel Zucker

Eating in the Underworld
The Last Clear Narrative
The Bad Wife Handbook

Women Poets on Mentorship: Efforts and Affections
(coedited with Arielle Greenberg)

MUSEUM
OF ACCIDENTS

rachel zucker

WAVE BOOKS

SEATTLE   NEW YORK

Published by Wave Books
www.wavepoetry.com

www.rachelzucker.net

Wave Books titles are distributed to the trade by
Consortium Book Sales and Distribution
Phone: 800-283-3572 / SAN 631-760X

This title is available in limited edition hardcover
directly from the publisher

Library of Congress Cataloging-in-Publication Data:
Zucker, Rachel.
 Museum of accidents / Rachel Zucker. — 1st ed.
    p. cm.
 ISBN 978-1-933517-42-1 (pbk. : alk. paper)
 I. Title.
 PS3626.U26M87 2009
 811'.6--dc22
                                    2009005831

Designed and composed by Stewart A. Williams
Printed in the United States of America

9 8 7 6 5 4 3 2 1

First Edition

Wave Books 019

for Josh

and for Matt Cruger
who taught us the difference between accidents and disasters

and for Moses, Abram and Judah

MUSEUM OF ACCIDENTS

THE DAY I LOST MY DÉJÀ VU

The box is like this today.
The box I live in.
Today: like this.

And though similar, so achingly alike,
ad infinitum, line over the nine, *again*,
it's always
nothing like
before,

nothing, not even the surprise
of another, so similar day of box-living.

Once, I was marked
and markedly different
and at times
while hopscotching
the grouted mosaic
felt *my god* I've seen
before a pattern
just like this

      I've been here!

But no more.

       now, I have never been anywhere
    elsc. ever but here and though I carry on
      can't return.

   even the day my firstborn son broke me
   opened and split shocked shattered that quaint notion of "before"

is no more than a rung of how I got
a mother's now-mind, a strung-together-bead's walk.

this moment. this. this. this.
                                        is not what I
                                        expected…

today my beautiful child eviscerates me.

a charmer, a snake, he fits my living heart
into his fist blunt fangs and I go willingly
                    into love with him. he is
every day a new child
and every day I'm still in love means
                    nothing like before.

                              remember when we
                              used to
remember
  things, every night, say
              remember the time…
        and the smells of the past and sometimes a portal
                                        opened up

and we slipped in there, into the past
            rose up to meet us we were not
    so all alone then, our lives had meaning
        and we were not born again every goddamn
    day but felt it what it felt like to be there
                in those lost places, the gone?

remember? those days? but I can't.

now all of me but this is gone and I was never a girl.

never but mother never

every same day new again. every way is without a way out or
way to look back, to *be* back, to bring the fabric into a tight
pucker or pocket or foxhole or hem, some little space to fall into a breath
like an open grave or little death. instead I learn bird names
for the shapes and colors and songs around me though every bird
is different from every bird. I learn the map. watch the armies advance,

forward! they bellow and jab mercilessly with their spear points,
go on!

carry! and so it is I haul my sons step after day each day so swept away by love
and terror I would sometimes rather kill us all than go on like this
marching, marching, new, new, new, day, and when they
are just too heavy to carry I become stronger
than is possible and carry on

3

WHAT DARK THING

The world is a place to buy things.

     Resist.

Even if it means your happiness.

Turn instead to the unmade choices, the others
like and not like you, the not-said, the stymied,
the scrim called day through which you make your way.

People have believed in God so long it must truly be
epidemic, this loneliness
even marriage can't quench and
babies aren't for company
only make you a mother
which is the last savage flower
on earth
not worth
buying.

Resist. Your happiness.

Question:

Are you the type of person who, when you hear a child suddenly died—
say a two and a half-year-old girl with a room full of toys—wants to have another?
                                    Just in case?

Or do you pull the mental picture of that room around you like sackcloth and tear
your hair?

If you think too hard about the number of people aboard the planet
you'll die.

                                        and well you should.

The room full of toys is a truck gliding by,
its side mirror catches you
unaware barely make a sound
as it slips you down, down skull
not so tough your brain fills
till the only way to save you is
induce coma you'll
never come out of—

                    pay attention.

This is not just the way you feel today. This is
the future retrospective portent that made it all
make sense.

Here is the formula to ward off tragedy:

Here is the antidote for despair:

Here is the only way to make it all make sense sooner:

                              but it won't.

What dark thing have you done to me?

Tuesday: therapy
Wednesday: mah-jongg
Thursday: we have sex (husband and I) lights on
frantic perhaps too much to wish for but more than nice a bit of
avalanche this time a cliff face along your body you have a body
while the computer goes to sleep flashing pristine beach scenes
I picture you and a young coed in a graduate carrel the girl
in a crisp button-down but her short short skirt she's over the table now
is so short her paisley underwear—

            What dark thing have you done to me?

Loved me and put aside the world.

These children.
Television.

"what I hear you saying is"

We learned to speak like that
in our inside voices while incessantly
sun-dressed women girls really to tell the truth babysitters and students
all the live wires electrodes walked by you didn't touch *don't touch!* but stayed with me
or at casinos with lowbrows and supported the DNC and Howard Dean and Noam
Chomsky and recycled and stopped sitting around in your half-open boxers and stopped
cutting onions with the wrong knife and putting the wooden spoons into the dishwasher
and using your fork like a dustbin and your fingers like a broom instead monogamy you
drove the car and carried the car seats and went out for NyQuil and Mallomars Children's
Motrin PediaCare diapers pull-ups baggies the other video and to return things that were
the wrong size or malfunctioned or mistaken or too easily broken you hung up the double
stroller carried the kids on your shoulders once in a while when I said *look at me* you did
and waited on the other side of the slammed door and took on my mother and made
mediocre lasagna when it was your turn to make dinner which was about five times in
seven years but that's five lasagnas and offered me ice cream which I hate but gave up
anchovy pizza and kept up with porn for all I know all I asked was for you to stop talking
about it and you did and the evidence went under wraps I assume there should be some
privacy don't you but you like the permeable membrane model of marriage the tell-all
forgive-all and really you gave me nothing that needed forgiveness and rather loved me
and put aside the world.

Come, thrust your strong beak into the solid floor of sky.
Hang on there and on until it stops. This love.

                              Obedience.

Here we stand: two naked participants: Pull.

Push. Hand and sigh. Do you
                              like this?

Uh-huh.

Roll over.
Trace this.
Rub this.
Slide this.
Soft this.

Hard hard hard slow slow slow then hard hard slow hard hard.
Do we do this and this and this.
You do that which I don't like anyway.

Roll
over. This way. Try this. Do you want to do this?

What about this? (More pillows.)

Can you sit up like this?

I thought you liked this…
OK?

Not enough. Dark.   Enough.

Where is my flesh ripper wrist holder abominable anti-
Christian narcissistic Neanderthal dark man

enough? Why can't you
take the body and make it sing
its pitiful rounds it is
not enough to take a woman
at face value or "be yourself"
i.e. married i.e. two people discrete sensible there is no sex
less possible than tender marriage without terror [or or or or].

I'd pay a thousand kopeks for a story I wouldn't believe.

But you can't do it because I believe everything,
have seen everything labeled and tagged and valued and sold.

Told and retold to a highest bidder.

We've kept the children safe. Our
vows. The lush and sunshiny world: we bought it.

Sometimes, at night, I wish I'd married Norman
Mailer and just once would like to make a man
riding by on a bike lose his balance
and die, make Mailer stop, mid-novel, to watch me
walking through Manhattan, buying nothing, not a thing.

Not happiness, not love, not the antidote or formula or trigger.
Not a pair of well-fitting jeans or self-esteem.

What dark thing, love, have you done to me?
Not dark enough.

WHEN ALL HANDS WERE CALLED TO MAKE SAIL

for Spalding Gray

The West and North winds both lover us, wanting, bitter,
to bring us in close in the small hold.

Tongues loll and laze, while the flap
and snapping above: crazy wanderlust.

The basin must cradle, keep her passengers,
though the hero abandoned the ferry for the real sea.

Is nothing worthy?

    Wallet on bench. Wallet at home. Wallet at rest.

The child, even his cries, must the ship balance,
makes me wild to right this unhumanly keeling.

I have six arms, am the dismembered figurehead,
ballast, breasts covered in blue scales.

I am at rudder, at bow, at mast, at rigging,
at deck, at halyard, at stern, when the hold

explodes with screaming.

One boy has stolen the other's marble. The boat shifts, tilts.
A wallet washes up against us.

Is this what you meant when you said a family steadied you?

Is this what they see when they see me and my six handless arms,
shining torso and cuspid humor?

The figurehead has no need for eyelids, must
on-guard, vigil, dry eyed.

But she dreams. Dreams.

The sail, its fine apparel, its linen long-shadow: a tiny hand
opening, budlike

LONG LINES TO STAVE OFF SUICIDE

One can live without having survived
Carolyn Forché

                                                            or
I could keep having children which helps a little (hurts
        a lot) because everything for a long time is so
keep-the-baby-alive,   or I
        could keep more to myself gathering
daily facts inwards in towards but this makes for
        less interior space
                if the line's
                too short
                drown—
too long—I'm not the first to be beguiled by and not the first to feel
                there's something [—hang—] I've swallowed that won't go down—

                                        on Thursday at pre-K
        I make pancakes with Abram's class and he asks Ami
and the teacher chose Luna and Derek cried and cried and I
        let him measure flour because he kept saying,
that's your mom? your mom? *I love your mom!* it was weird
        so I gave him butter and a blunt knife, hoped the teacher
wouldn't mind and later found out Derek's mom
        died in the towers

        I couldn't breathe when I heard it or believe what a good mother
I've been just by staying alive

do you think? Joan asks, *it's better to die now or back when they were babies*
and didn't know better? I almost say better to have died when they were babies
        but. not true. every good night book. spoon of puréed pear. banana
after brush-your-teeth time. how I held him (restrained in a hospital sheet)
        while the idiot doctor who didn't want to dirty his dress shirt
stitched the busted lip. and when I weaned him off the binky and the boob
        and the floaties and from biting and kicking and unbuttoning my shirt
in public and from climbing out of the crib and from standing up on the subway
        without holding on—*better, I say, to*

                                    die now

                            or,

when he reaches an age
        (what age?) and I find I can finally swallow it down—will I?
                                            loosen?

perhaps if I can get the color just right in my study I will not need to stand
        in the back of the synagogue and miss the shofar again this year
but it's not right, too light, like springtime. gray-green not gray
        or green. not yellow. not blue. it will not do have I done this
on purpose? picked the color of the inside of a seed I should never have opened?

                        …where is my breath is…

can barely hear above the clicking of my thinking why

        am I so obsessed with paint color and the properties of seasons

material objects I'm crazy so lazy and *driven*, relentless, no one could stand this

        they call it cyclical negative thinking the constant self-checking

am I okay now? now? now? worse? better? now?

        above the well-deserved charge of narcissism, above the thrum

of how many people alive now and now how many dead. I've not read

        the *New York Times* for four years and one month but it hasn't helped.

                      or would I be

           worse?

        every touch too much but *imperceptible* perhaps a fever somewhere? and

people dying faster than I can write poems.

                 when my students want to write poems

        I want to say wait for everyone to die.

instead I say: *the poem must have a surprise and needs images*

        and where are the things? the real world matters. one fish

in a barrel of fish. one bird in a flock of birds.

        was it a bass?

    a blue jay?

oh, for fuck's sake, there's no difference between "stones" and "rocks" in Virginia's

        frock. down, down, down into the world of objects

which the students haven't got
                has nearly killed me.

my son has a dream. cries. is afraid to tell me.
later he says that many, many people
came into his room at night all missing
something: an eye, an arm, a leg, a head
he knew them by their voices instead
and did *not* like what they were saying

I have everything. even a job.
                a child. a child. notebooks I cannot quite
get down.

why, asks my son on the subway, *should you*
                say *something if you* see *something?*
pointing at the poster of an abandoned black
                duffel on a subway platform. I am trying
to breathe but he's asking and pointing. I say,
                birds don't have teeth and need to eat
small rocks, stones, sand to break down food. he
                nods, pats my hand.

I'm trying so hard not to show him
                my worldview I can barely breathe. gave him
a brother want to give him another and never
                tell him there are things
and things that explode and no easy way to know
                the difference. I drop him off at school, go to class
where the students say something and say
                something and rarely see anything.

                                I wonder,
what if the black bag is filled with not-bombs? filled with

long, smooth seeds surprisingly soft to the touch
each containing a human baby? shall I swallow one
                                        down?

This morning, alone,
            I'm listening to music so as not to hear
the explosion
            if there is one certainly eventually will be one
(today an alert)
            every moment is not *yet*
exploded or gaseous or biological,
            not yet infectious. *should I*
not *ride the subway?* I ask. the husband:
            you've felt pretty low lately
anyway. we both laugh.

In class a student says, *living in a metropolis is good because it helps you have an*
open mind which is good so you're not ignorant.

            so here I am again with 8,168,388 people.

            Good morning, I don't say to anyone, I'm experiencing panic. And
depression. No, actually, nothing's wrong but thanks for the Kleenex. Sometimes
            the subway sets it off. Or the bus. Elevator. Small spaces. The vacuum
cleaner. Ambient radio. Things inside other things as if myself a Russian doll or
            that everyone has masks my unmedicated eye can't help but notice—

I like short lines, says a student.
I like poems without images, says a student.

I wanted everything to sound very superficial, says a student.
You never said it had to be interesting, says a student.

I want someone to ask me if I like my job.

I want someone to explain why I put a large duffel bag of explosives
        into my mouth and tried to swallow it down when I was just
trying to stay alive, terrified my sons could see my missings, and how is it the cops
        don't stop me and my open-minded subway neighbors smile sweetly
as we hurtle along and I tell my jostling boys, *no, no you must hold on, hold on,*
        any moment it could stop, suddenly, stop
                        short, I must

    hold on.

HEY ALLEN GINSBERG WHERE HAVE YOU GONE AND WHAT WOULD YOU THINK OF MY DRUGS?

listen, a bad thing happened to
my friend's marriage, can't tell you
only can tell my own story which
so far isn't so bad:

"Dad" and I stay married. so far.
so good. so so.

But it felt undoable. This lucky life
every day, every day. every. day.

(all the poetry books the goddamn same
until one guy gets up and stuns the audience.)

Joe Wenderoth, not by a long shot
sober, says, *I promised my wife I wouldn't fuck
anyone* to no one in particular and reads a poem
about how Jesus had no penis.

Meanwhile, the psychiatrist, attractive
in a fatherly way, says, *Libido* question mark.

And your libido?
like a father, but not like mine, or my sons'—

fix it.

My friend Nathan's almost written
a good novel, by which I mean finished,
which means I'd like to light myself
on fire—this isn't "desire,"

not what the Dr. meant
by libido?

                    I hope—

not, it's just chemical:
           jealousy. boredom. lethargy.

Books with prominent serifs: their feet feet feet I am
marching to the same be—

other

than the neuronic slave I thought anxiety made me
do it, made me get up and carry forth, sally
the children to school the poems dragged
by little hands on their little serifs
to the page, my marriage sustained, remaining
energy: project #1, project #2, broken
fixtures, summer plans, demands met, requests
granted, bunny noodles with and without cheesy
at the same time, and the nighttime, I insomnia
these hours penning invisible letters—

           till it stopped.

doc said: *It's a syndrome. You've got it,*
                  classic.

It's chemical,
mental

circuitry, we've got a fix for this
classic, I'm saying I can

make it better.

Everything was the same, then,
but *better.*

At night I slept.
In the morning got up.

Kids to school, husband still a fool-
hardy spirit makes
me pick a Monday morning fight, snipe! I'll pay for that
later I'm still a pain in the
elbow from writing prose those shift+hold+letter,
I'm still me less sleepy, crazy, I suppose
less crazy-jealous just
haha now at Jesus' no penis
amazed at the other poet's kick-ass
friend's novel I dream instead about
the government makes me put stickers
on my driver's license of family members
who are Jews, and mine all are. Can they get us
all? I escape with a beautiful light-haired man,
blue-eyed day trader, gentile.

                              ((gentle, gentle, mind encased in its
                              blood-brain barrier from the harsh skull
                              sleep, sleep and sleepy wake and want
                              to sleep and sleep a steep dosage—

                                   "—chemical?"))

in my dreams now every man's mine, no
problem, perhaps my mind's a little plastic,

20

malleable, not so fatal now

the dose is engineered like that new genetic watercress
to turn from green to red when planted over buried
mines, nitrogen dioxide makes for early autumn,
red marks the spot where I must
watch my step, up one half-step-dose specific—

The psychiatrist's lived in NY so long
he's of ambiguous religious—
everyone's Jewish sometimes—
writes: "Up the dosage."

       ((now,
       when I'm late I just shrug
       it's my new improved style
       missed the train? I tug
       the two boys single file

       the platform a safe aisle
       between disasters, blithely
       I step, step, step lively
       carefully, wisely

       I sing silly ditties
       play I spy something pretty-
       gray-brown-metal-filthy
       for a little city fun

       just one way to enjoy life's
       trials, mile after mile, lucky
       to have such dependable feet

       you see, the rodents
       don't frighten I'm calm

          as can be expected to recover
          left to my own devices I was
          twice as fast getting everywhere but where
          did that get me but, that inevitable location
          more waiting, the rats there scurry, scurry, a furry
          till the next train comes—))

"Up the dosage."

Brown a first-cut brisket in hot Dutch oven
after dusting with paprika. Remove. Sauté
thickly sliced onions and add wine (sweet
is better, lasts forever, never need a new bottle).
Put the meat on onions, cover with tomato-sauce-
onion-soup-mix mixture, cover. Back in low oven
many hours.

This year, I'll be better;
trying to get out of Egypt.

The house smells like meat.
My hair smells like meat.

I'm a light unto the nation.

Joseph makes sense of the big man's dreams, is saved,
saves his brothers those jealous boys who sold him
sold them all as slaves. Seven years of plenty. Seven
years of famine. He insomnias the nights counting up
grains, storing, planning, for what? They say throw
the small boys in the river (and mothers do so). Smite
the sons (and fathers do it). God says take off your shoes,
this holy ground this pitiful, incombustible bush.

Is God chemical?
Enzymatic of our great need to chaos?

We're unforgivable. People of the salted
cheeks. Slap, turn, slap.

To be chosen is to be
unforgiving/unforgiv-
en, always chosen:
be better.

The Zuckers are a long line of obsessives.

This served them well in wartime saw it
coming in time that unseeable thing they
hoarded, they ferried, schemed, paced, got the hell
out figured out at night, insomnia, how to visa—

now, if it happens again, I won't be
ready—

I'm "better."

The husband, a country club Jew from Denver,
American intelligentsia, will have to carry me out
and he's no big man and I'm
not a small girl how fast…

can the doctor switch the refugee gene back on?

How fast can I get worse? Smart again and worse?

It is better to be alive than better.

...*Listen:* says the doctor, *Sleeping isn't death.*
All children unlearn this fear you got confused
thought thinking was the same as—
Writes: "Up the dosage."

Don't think. this refugee thing part
of a syndrome fear of medication of being better...

Truth is, the anti-obsessional medicine works
wonders and drags me through life's course.

Light unto the Nation.

About this time of year but years ago
the priests spread rumors of blood libel.
Jews huddled in basements accused
of using Christian babes' blood
to make unleavened bread.

Signs and wonders.
Christ rises.

Blood and body and babes.
Basements and briskets
and bread of afflictions.

[I] am calm now with my pounds of meat
made and frozen, my party schedule, my pills
of liberation, my gentile dream-boy, American
passport, my gray-haired psychiatrist, my blue-
eyed son, my brown-eyed son, my poems on their
pretty little fleet-feet, my big shot friends, olive-skinned
husband, my right elbow on fire: fire inside deep in the nerve
from too much carrying and word-mongering, smithery, bearing

and tensing, choosing to be better to live this real life this better orbit this Jack

Kerouac never loved you like you wanted—

Blake.
Buddha.
Only Jesus and that's his shtick,
he loves

everyone: smile! that's it,
for the camera, blood pressure
normal, *better*, you're a poster child
for signs and wonders what a little chemistry
does for the brain, blood, thoughts, hey,

did you know that Pharaoh actually *wanted*
to let them go? those multitude Jews
but God hardened Pharaoh's heart against them [Jews]
to prove his prowess, show his signs, wonders, outstretched
hand, until the dosage was a perfect ten and then
some, sea closing up around those little chariots
the men and horses while women on the far shore shook
their tambourines. And then what?

                                              Forty years
to get the small of slavery off them.

Because of this. Bloody Nile. My story
one of the lucky. Escape hatch even from
my own obsess—

                              I am here because of this.
Because of what my ancestors did for me to tell this
story of the outstretched hand what it did for me this

marked door and behind this red-marked door, around
a corner a blue-eyed boy waits to love me up with his
leavened bread, his slim body, professional detachment,
medical advancements, forgive me my father's mother's
father was the last in a long line of rabbis—again! with this? This
rhapsody of affliction and escape, the mind bobbing along
in its watery safe. Be like everyone. Else. Indistinguishable but
better than the other nations. But that's what got us into this, Allen,
no one writes these long-ass poems anymore. Now we're
better, all better. All Christian. Kind.

TO SAVE AMERICA

1.
I'm tired of watching Kennedy die. and I

'm tired of J. Jr. in the pinafore and of innocence
and of saying we didn't know
deserve desire get exactly what we

wished for—oh, let's not go down
to Dallas; instead

let's get booed.

2.
when one encounters this animal there will be
a great flood
when one encounters this animal there will be
a terrible epidemic
when one encounters this animal there will be
holocaust
when one encounters this animal there will be
catastrophe

it is a cannibal
it is a cannibal
it is a cannibal
it is

3.
in here, where
civilians not allowed

4.
did you pack it yourself?
has it always been in your possession?
was it ever beyond your control?
did anyone ever give you anything?
is anything wrapped?
are there electronics?
do you have any gifts?

5.
yes: I have the 1st photo after the end of America.

would you care to unwrap it?
hang it in your cockpit?

6.
According to Ad Reinhardt Ad Reinhardt's black paintings
were the last paintings anyone could make. At least
the last black paintings. Good

poetry blew the top of Dickinson's
head off and according to Ginsberg would

save America. The poem

7.
once thought to be a grassy knoll
is often mistaken for a bulletproof
door but may be just another black

painting so open it: release the fanged
animal America that can unsave this
president who's never had his

head blown off. Do it—due to
turbulence the masks suddenly fallen—
grasp—gasp—open the door barely muffling
the tripped alarm

8.
save America save America
from the little self save
America save America save
self save self from self from
save from save from America
save from safe America self
safe America self safe America
self ave ave ave
ave ave ave ave ave ave
ave av av av of of of
of of of of of of of of of
of [vav] [vav] [vav] [vav]
of [vav] [vav] [vav] [vav]
of [vav] [vav] [vav] [vav]
of of save of save. save of
save. safe of save. save.
safe of save. save. save
of safe. safe. safe. safe.
safe. safe. safe. safe. safe.
safe. safe. safe. safe. safe.
safe. safe. safe. safe. safe.
safe. safe. of _____
_____
_____ of
    off.

NICE ARSE POETICA

Nothing happened.

And not because I'm sometimes grouped
with those e[x]peri(mental) poets, I mean it

when I say: I didn't [ ]
anyone (kiss him)—hold on, once
I told a class, *Remember, "experimental"*
means "based on experience," from middle
English, Latin, middle French. "Experience" means
"to try" or "participation in events
as a basis of knowledge;" "something personally
encountered, undergone, lived through."

                                                  uh-oh…

Did? (something) have? happen?

o hap! by chance, a hapless chap so lucky to have loved and lost and all that. Crap,
        did I?

To "coy" means "to caress" so use the adjective instead:
"bashful, shy, demure, marked by playful artlessness—"

nothing happen
                    ed—bat, bat my lashes—to say or do otherwise is just
bad form not what poems are for so for god's sake find yourself
a confessional.

They say a sin
must be actual

to be mortal so,
though in peril,
I aver: nothing
happened. you'll find
no *there* there nor
novel here. no fangled plot
device. only: cries
of the occasion, objective
correlatives and otherwise
just language play and no one
ever got a baby that way

or did they?

Hello Beckett. Hello chastity. Hello great saints and nuns, monks
and mendicants. Hello vegans and flagellants. Hello all ye grand
regretters. Middle-aged Americans with TiVo lest you miss, by god,
miss an episode, the one where such and such happened. "Cheers!"
to all who imagine ourselves worthy of happenings. Worthy of waiting.
Needing. Wanting. Hello longing. Hello Neruda. Hello Christians waiting for Christ
to come back. Hello applause between the curtain and encore. Hello strange culture
that pays men to punch each other until one falls down. Hello Tristan on his deathbed
waiting, whispering, *please, please, what color are the sails?* Hello Isolde of the White Hands
who saw the raised white sails and said, *o love, my love, the sails are black.* Knowing it
would kill him, her beloved man, for she could not abide his love for the better-loved
Isolde the Fair.

Hello memory. Hello childhood. Hello Middle Ages and Milan Kundera.
Vladimir Nabokov and Norman Mailer. Hello novels and plot progression
and movements and manifestos. Hello pregnant pauses. Hello active labor.
Hello ringing telephone. Hello to all things waiting to happen. I'm sorry

to disappoint you.

Just a poem   after all…

                                                        Move along. Move along. Nothing
                                                                to see here.

Excuse me?

Did you say my soul
mattered? My heart's delight? My roving
eye?

To whom?

I'm alive. Aren't I?

Not struck down yet. Paul Valéry said poetry
was language that did not die for having lived but I say
poems are too like the lightning which doth cease to be ere one can say
"It lightens." It strikes me:

He did have a terribly nice arse.
Callipygian in his ready-to-wear.

Oh, for shame. A shande.

What would I want with a shaygets, some nonjewboy with a shayne punim
worth all this tsuris like a special on Lifetime or O TV? What does any nice girl
like me

want?

My sweet husband would have told the truth as the ship hurled itself
to harbor. As would I. *White sails.* The sails were white. Doth our honesty mean
our love's less epic or more true? What's it to you

if nothing happened? What does it prove? That inaction is the sole measure left
to those bound up in monotony I mean monogamy?

Assignment: Write a nice experimental poem in which nothing happens based on
something you have personally encountered, lived through, undergone.

Haply I think on thee.

But why compare?
I'm "wife!" Stop there!

My husband, just so's you know, keeps our cash in *Etiquette* by Emily Post
between *On Lies, Secrets, and Silence* and *An Anthology of New Poetics.* He's sure to be
pissed at me for this and other indiscretions.

Before literature? Before artfulness?
Was there ever a time when privacy existed?

Tryst (*triste*) from Middle French: watch post.
Tryst (*traust*) from Old Norse: to trust.

No wonder he's pissed off.

But see here, the LexisNexis search swears to my fidelity
says I've been exactly nowhere with no one at least once.
And even had I been otherwise, a poem's not the place to do "it," no,

here's just me and my Diaspora, me and my metaphysical alienation,
me and my fragmented self, battered and fraught with motifs of loss
and loneliness, longing, and of course that irritable reaching, reaching after, after

after a little of what all true misery loves…

WELCOME TO THE BLIGHTED OVUM SUPPORT GROUP

the well-timed hanger joke

took the air out of the room
so that the instruments pulled at their cords
and my gurney leaned on its wheels
and the residents stopped scratching
the bands of their surgical caps
to look in wonder
that the husband
could have been
so crude

Dr. Jew

was the G.Y.N.'s
real name. no kidding—
spelled: J.E.W.

my hospital bracelet:

RACHEL ZUCKER
1 2 / 2 7 / 7 1
J E W

---

was a kind man, held my hand
asked after my children, said, *I'm sorry
this is happening,* and left a nickel-sized
piece of tissue that made me
bleed for weeks until I

                              couldn't stand
                              up the world
                              a swaying back-
                              drop all
                              around and
                              around and
                              the medication
                              failed and the meditation
                              and Maya massage
                              and folded prayer I put
                              in the real wailing wall
                              and herbs and acupuncture
                              and waiting until
                              we went back to our places,
                              all of us: residents, jokers,
                              instruments, though this
                              time through the ER,
        so there were other characters and indecencies and I became aware of

how the air was sucked out of all the rooms

              aware of how little air there'd been for weeks
and not just because hospital and residents who say *abortion*
              which is technically correct and the nurse with bad
English who leaned in close to what? hug me? her breath
              in my ear

              the only air,

he hurt you?

           can barely hear the words didn't make sense, *who?*

    he!

          she's adamant—

heee, heee!

          says the nurse at the closed door behind which the husband—

no, no, I say, *he not hurt me,*

                   and she misses the vein
          and flicks at the tube, does it again and again until
             the needle finds a rivulet and hunkers down to pump

the joke I make at her expense keeps us moving through space
         and time and able to lie still when it is time
and time to wait for the procedure, until a different nurse,
         all pink-cheeked and matronly, comes in and asks,

how many weeks along?

    and no one has a joke ready, for this; there isn't one

she thinks we haven't heard, says,

pregnant… how many weeks? and I,

I'm here for a second D&C because the first D&C after a missed miscarriage
due to blighted ovum resulted in heavy bleeding for the past six weeks now I can
barely stand up and last night thought I am finally bleeding to death and Arielle
said, oh god this doesn't sound good, maybe you should lie down, bleeding like
that… I mean women have babies when they sit on the toilet… I mean the

bleeding might be worse there because of gravity and, I don't know, maybe go to the hospital? and Arielle hates hospitals so you know oh god it really did not sound good and I did lie down with my hips up and did not bleed to death at least not yet though there's always a risk with any surgical procedure and no guarantee the D&C will address this bleeding unless a piece of tissue the uterus can't expel and Dr. Jew can get it out now but it's tricky because they can't see anything on the sono except my uterus isn't empty that's what they keep saying "your uterus isn't empty" but they can't see could be tissue could be clots but to answer your question not, they're sure, a baby, maybe never was all they saw at 11.5 weeks was a hearty placenta and empty sac the placenta supporting no fetus and pumping me full of progesterone so I was terrifically morning sick and popped out in maternity clothes convinced a healthy baby maybe a girl this time why else so sick and big and happy…

but that's not the punch line to anyone's joke
                              and not what I said. I said

        look at the chart in a cracked voice and
                              she did, said, *oh.*
                      not the least bit abashed, walked away

                                              no one has a joke about her.

I wish I'd said, sixteen weeks and five days fuck you very much, or something, anything, but nothing came to us, out of comebacks, even the husband, my crude beauty, for once, without a punch line.

WELCOME TO THE BLIGHTED OVUM SUPPORT GROUP.

They say "lost" a baby.

The technician says:
This is the sac.
This is the placenta.

This is your bladder and one, and another
ovary. Nothing, I'm afraid.
Else.

Empty

       sac.

The placenta just kept on HCG. Have to pee be
sick. protein. sick. protein. told everyone. the boys.

_____ sac.

naughty fetus, hiding like that.
or invisible or neverwas.

uterine wall.

the unfetus or preembryo. scaffold, sac, yolk.

How do you feel knowing you'll write about this?

the husband asks two days after the first sonogram
is the first time someone
asks me how I feel

○

I take *Ignatia* for grief.
Aconite for shock.
Chamomilla for anger which out of nowhere like a slap.
Herbs for retained placenta.
Needles for retained placenta.
Needles for weak pulse, for grief, for shock, for disappointment.

I drink wine, coffee and take pills except
I don't, not yet, just in case.

In case hiding. In case mistaken.

Wait. Waiting.

Let go, I tell the placenta. Go.
Go now.

        but had lost nothing. would let nothing go, nothing.

The next sono shows the placenta breaking down
and the sac misshapen, deflating?

Nothing was changed then except information.
Still no bleeding, sign, nothing. Not
a baby for weeks or ever
but in a few days, after I see the empty sac,
my belly starts to shrink.
I wash and fold the maternity clothes
to return to their rightful owners. My son
erases the part in his family narrative that says
"_____ is my_____."

I'd rather write poems about a baby, is how I feel, you motherfucker.

O

In the prose version I write eloquently about
how important it is for my sons to feel
disappointment like this and survive.

In verse I write nothing, which is
an objective correlative of what I've "lost."

When Nathan calls I cannot
get up. His voice sounds like
his voice like nothing's
happened. Sitting with the *Post*
at the Pastry, wants to know
if I'll come translate
an Ancient Hebrew poem, but
I can't get up.

can only troll the Web for tales more dismal than my own
and there are
many.

WELCOME TO THE BLIGHTED OVUM SUPPORT GROUP.
THERE ARE 3 NEW MEMBERS.

WELCOME: THERE ARE 4 NEW MEMBERS.

They say the first thing I asked
after the procedure was,

What was in there?
when I was still on the table
but I've no memory of anything before Recovery
where I woke up crying.

Picture every alien abduction movie
where they experiment on earthlings:
that is the O.R.

Umbrella-sized movable lights like obscene poppies,
fabric stirrups hanging from the ceiling:
Slide your bottom down… down… down, no, too much…

I'm crying.
Dr. Jew holds my hand.
It's hard to have it all be over, I say
not knowing then that when I wake up
it will not be over.

at first everyone says, *sorry you lost a baby,*
and my father has a nightmare: he's riding
a city bus and sees something beautiful
through the window but can't get off
and strange hands come to snatch it away—

he is sorry I lost the baby
and my sons weeping—

the older: *I can't take this*—
the younger: *but where did it go?*—

and some mother at the school says
that's why you shouldn't say anything

for at least 13 weeks it's so
easy
to lose
a baby—

But I didn't.

I held on and on to the sac had to have it
scraped out then could not stop bleeding
the shots and pills and herbs and pellets
even a woman singing and praying over my uterus
and others lighting candles for me, saying,
you need to let it go now

      whatever's left just let it go

I could not believe
what bloody else
could be left
I'd let everything
          go
     until fell
down
and stayed
down, stoned-like
whoosh
goes the world
filling the toilet
blood advice
      no one
knows
what
swirling
the stream of it

if I can't have the baby what have I—

O

When I looked in the notebooks there was nothing there.

I assumed I'd been writing things down and poems would tumble out.

Instead I found instructions about what to do for back labor:
"Assume a semi-prone position, or knees lower than hips, then lie on the side of the baby."

Fuck the notebooks.

C took her embryo to the doctor's office in a Tupperware.
A had a perfectly good baby stuck in her fallopian tube they used chemo because "any fast-growing
    cell" but had to blow her up like a balloon and take it out laparoscopically when the tube burst
    anyway.
B had a rush of bleeding while teaching.
P's water breaks at 16 weeks on her way back from the Cape.
J has a miscarriage in an airport bathroom.

They sustain me with stories so gory I was almost envious back when I was still waiting
for something still technically pregnant but without a baby and not one drop of blood or
pain to show for it finally agreed to the first D&C because "a relatively predictable
outcome" and I was flying to Israel and wouldn't want to end up in hospital so Dr. Jew
nice Asian man holds my hand, I say *it's hard for it to all be over* thinking it would be
and he says he's sorry this is happening and I wake up in Recovery crying and they say
expect spotting and the husband and I get drunk and go out dancing because we are still
alive and I've had a procedure which has given us closure and we fly to Israel and the
bloodletting begins and nothing will stop it and I'm in the middle of my own very gory

story but too anemic to write it up properly for the all ladies who are waiting and waiting to miscarry or for their procedures who have dead fetuses or empty sacs inside them or are trying to conceive or are pre- or post-D&C or are writing to say this is the anniversary of the EDD for the neverwas baby and they are calling themselves angel mothers and I am too weak to be snide about this and they are arguing about whether a woman can post to the list who has recently had a miscarriage but not from blighted ovum if she's had three blighted ovum pregnancies in the past

THERE ARE 4 NEW MEMBERS.
THERE IS 1 NEW MEMBER.
THERE ARE 5 NEW MEMBERS.

WELCOME.

I'll tell you all what happened, properly and in order, when I'm not so dizzy, if I'm ever more with it, when the bleeding stops and it hits me what I've lost, when sadness finally gets up the nerve to come calling and settles like a scab where they've scraped away the last nickel-sized piece of tissue, a scab too easily dislodged by the sight of pregnant women or newborns or thoughts of last New Year's Eve when we watched the fireworks from our apartment naked after saying and doing crude things to each another and making what would not be born October 1st or worse, the moment we had no answer for how many weeks along when we'd lost everything even our last rusty-hanger abortion joke—

how many weeks?

One, but the lightbulb really has to want to change.
Goldberg, iceberg—what's the difference?
Three: two to hold down the giraffe and one to kiss the fish.
Oy, vas I tirsty!
Stupid genie thought I asked for a 12-inch pianist.
Would I! Would I!… Hair lip! Hair lip!
That? That could lead to dancing.

Keys, wallet, spectacles, testicles.
Bok? Bok?... Readit. Readit
I said, Go down on the wharf!
Don't worry, Rose, it's something to do with the gentiles.
Because seven ate nine.
The phone's for you, cocksucker.

PAYING DOWN THE DEBT: HAPPINESS

At the end of my second book is a poem about my second son's birth
called "Here Happy Is No Part of Love." It's a raw poem, full of the sounds
    and smells and terrors of labor. About going to a place I swear I cannot go.
Going there alone. Going unwillingly. Surviving. Surviving to build a nest
    with shards of glass. Happiness, the poem says, is a frail, wispy emotion
that has no part in the fierce love of birth and motherhood. Happiness can't touch
    the molten heart of motherhood. Happiness is irrelevant to these maternal
fires and by the way I wasn't (as if that mattered) happy by the way didn't want
    (at least so soon) another child. Well, at readings people are always tsk-tsking although
mothers are also nodding and sometimes crying but at least one person
    from every audience comes up to me and says, *you'll pay for that. Someday,*
he'll grow up and read that and you'll pay.

So I'm working away on a book of prose. A nonfiction book about motherhood.
A "momoir" as they call it in that already saturated momlit pub market. And I'm
    suffering. Suffering through every word of this goddamn book, yelling
at the computer and lying on the bed crying and generally carrying on. Meanwhile,
    because it is nonfiction, I'm caught in a weird hell of having to live my life twice
every day. Struggle through the writing of my life and then the kids come home
    and I have to take care of them having had a bad writing morning and feeling like a
failure and *no I do not want to do a Batman puzzle* and *no I do not want to watch you*
    fold another paper airplane and *no I do not want to play knights or superheroes or*
Star Wars or Legos please stop hitting your brother or I'm going to take those lightsabers away I
    don't have the yogurt that turns blue because I didn't go to the grocery store because I was writing
anyway I'm not going to buy that yogurt that turns blue because it's gross, it's gross because
    it's not natural it has preservatives, preservatives are chemicals they put in food to make it
stay good longer but we should eat foods that are fresh and don't have preservatives, there are dyes
    and chemicals in that and I'm not getting it because it's disgusting, yeah well Ava's mom is not your mom, yes,
blueberries are blue but they're blue naturally, no, I don't have blueberries because I
    didn't go to the grocery store and anyway they're not in season now, "in season" means that fruits and
vegetables grow at certain times of year and now it's March almost no berries grow this time of year,

no I don't have strawberries, no yogurt doesn't have a season, look I'm going to go make
dinner now, noodles, because that's what we have because I didn't go to the grocery store because I
was writing.

The next morning hurry them to school, come home because I have a schedule
　　　and this book is not getting done on its own, there is never a time I want to
write it, and the grocery store will have to wait we have frozen peas and noodles
　　　and I suffer through another thousand words keeping to the schedule. Then to school,
gather them home, and try to speak to them kindly but feeling like my skin
　　　is too tight, like I'm the mother in smothered.

Motherhood has taken my *I* and smothered her to smithereens. I'm bothered.
　　　　　Hot. Lusty. Restless.

　　　　　　　　　　　　Then, it happens. My son Moses looks up at me all pink-
　　　　cheeked and sweet, sweet, sweet-faced and I know:

　　　by evening I can feel his fever across the room. Nighttime he is nuclear, radiant,
a febrile jewel emitting a strange honeyed smell. Saturday. Sunday. Monday. Tuesday.
　　　There is no more writing. We are smothered together. No more school.
Smother. No more schedule. Smothered. Tuesday. Wednesday. Thursday. I read him
　　　every King Arthur book in the library. At night dream of sweet adultery
with Gawain, Lancelot, Griflet, Tristram, Pellinore, and several Saxon kings.
　　　I refuse only Galahad as he is too pure for me. And no one blames me.
It's my destiny. *Finally, finally,* says Merlin, stroking my brow, *thanks to you,*
　　　there is peace in Britain.

　　　When I wake up I am sick. I am a flame-breathing dragon and for my sins
of the flesh my flesh is punished. Moses goes to school and I am left to sweat

and shiver through the day. Friday. Saturday. My mother is in Vietnam.
My father and stepmother are in Israel. My husband is the world's greatest
　　　heroine for taking the children to a birthday party then the park then to a movie
so I can, abandoned at home, burn at the stake in privacy. Bath, bed, bath. Bed,
　　　bed, bed. Tea, bed, bed. Bath, bed, bed. My head. My chest. My eyes. My skin.

At 6 p.m. the front door lock turns, all hail the retreating armies. *GAS!* the husband bugles.
GAS! GAS! GAS! I can smell it down the hall! I stagger forth and with my hoarse
　　　voice say, *You know, I'm really sick of your hyperbolic, psychosomatic hypochondriacal bullshit!*
And he: *The house is filled with gas. Sylvia Plath–gas! You can't smell it?*
　　　Smell? But when I enter the kitchen I see it's true: I've left the gas, sans flame,
running for at least three hours. The husband darts room to room opening windows,
　　　glaring. *At least the kids weren't here,* I say. The four of us go sit in the hallway
for half an hour while the neighbors sniff and stare accusingly.

Sunday morning I wake in a cold sweat. Fever breaks: I'm smithered. Three hours
later a client calls to say she's in labor can I now, right now, please, to Cornell
　　　Weil Hospital? I arrive at noon. Lunge. Stairs. Squat. Breathe, squat, lunge. Breathe,
stairs, hip press. Squeeze, cry: *Please. No, no, no.* Breathe, hold, hold. Push,
　　　push, push. Push, push, push. Push, push, push. *No, please, no.* More, more. More.
Can't breathe more more more more more. Fourteen hours later she has her baby.

At 4 a.m. I return home to find the husband awake and none too pleased.
He's stayed up late playing online poker and has a stomachache. Recently we have
　　　stopped fighting in couple's therapy about online poker because we've stopped going
to couples therapy because my son has stopped going to school and all our
　　　babysitters are in foreign countries. Smother……. Smother. So I say, *So sorry
about your stomach maybe you shouldn't have stayed up so late* and he: *Don't make this about
　　　poker* and I: *OK* and we go to bed and one hour later hear: *Dad… Dad…
Dad…………………… Dad… Dad…* and you know of course it is the faint
　　　frail voice of my younger son my god there will be no schedule nor writing,
not sleep, and the creep, "Dad," yells, *Go back to sleep!*
　　　　　　　　　　Don't yell at him, I yell.
　　　　　　　　　　　　Don't yell at me, he yells
and Abram has 102°

The Muppet Show is too singy. *The Jungle Book* is too quiet. *The Lion King* is too loudly. The Super Friends are so boring. *Star Wars* is too fighty. He will not let me. Sleep. Please, please, please, please. He will not let me. I hold him in my arms and pace up and down and back and forth through the long minutes of Monday

morning. While other children of other mothers are going to school. While other mothers are doing what other mothers are doing. And I know I'm not alone

in the path I furrow in the rug of morning and all over the world mothers are back and forth with babes in arms and I call out to them in a smothered whisper

and the morning shifts just a bit, a bit, like steam coming off a long highway on a hot day, the world straining a bit under the silent weight of my comrade in

arms' response. Heavy. He is four years old, I tell the other mothers. I am trying to make him comfortable but he is not a baby. I have no breast. He will take nothing:

drink nor eat nor song nor sleep. Mothers, I call out, it is Monday and Monday and Monday and still Monday and my arms are not so strong anymore.

I put him in the stroller for someone will need to pick up Moses. Abram falls instantly to sleep. The day creeps on. Out on Broadway I walk the minutes away. I

sit down on a hydrant in the winter sun to rest, just rest, feel that sun on me. I think that I have never been outside before, is it possible? I think I've been forever

in mortal combat with the computer or deep in hospital with the infernal fetal monitor, wizard's drum beat marching us on, and in the school with its gray light,

and grocery store with people feeding and feeding and buying food about to go bad or filled with chemicals or in bookstores to give readings or in libraries touching

the acetate spines like holy tablets for a story to save us and in the sick room where me and Charlotte Perkins Gilman are stroking each other's damp brows

goading each other on but here, here on Broadway, slumped in the sun on the hydrant I feel, for a moment, free. Warm. Happy?

A woman stops to look down at my fallen boy-knight, his cherry-bright lips. So precious, he is barely of this world, his skin so pale barely hides what lies beneath.

In Korea we say all the work you do for your kids their whole life they pay you back the first year. You see? She points at my son. The audience nods. Smiles, knowingly.

The boy wakes and whines, *Make it move, Mama. Make it move.* And I do. Walk. Walk on. Walk through. Happiness is for sissies, I tell the mothers of the furrow.

Happiness is for chumps and weaklings and martyrs. I walk up Broadway

through the city of the world. The trusty steed. The lance. The shield. I fight on
        without any. Arthur, you prefer the sword? It is the scabbard you should precious.
As long as you wear it you'll not perish from wounds. Pierced, I laugh
        in the face of happiness. Happiness, that smoky potion fit for fools and rogues
and those susceptible to vanity. Come, let the Great Green Knight bring sharpened
        sword down upon my nape. But for a thin line of blood I will not break.

        In the cab ride home from school the boys kick each other with maleficence.
Kick and punch and scrabble. *I am trying to teach you COMPASSION*, I scream.
        The driver checks his mirrors. *And if you cannot learn COMPASSION I will
punish you both so severely that—*

                                Is that my destiny, Mama? asks one son, calmly.
                        To be punished severely?

        At home the husband, having awoken from a long nap, is nonplussed to see us.
Abram begs for cereal. *No! You're sick,* says the husband.
                                Don't yell at him, I yell.
                                Don't yell at me, he yells.

        He brings Abram cereal. *Milk!* yells Abram. *No! You're sick, no milk,* says the husband.
Give him rice milk, I hiss. *But that's disgusting,* he says. *Don't say that
        in front of the kids,* I say. *Whatever,* he says. A few minutes later I see him pouring
organic free-range chicken broth over Abram's cereal by mistake. I can't even say
        what I said.

Smother. Smother. Smother. The apartment is smithereened. The *I* is paid out. Almost.

Uppy, uppy, uppy, uppy, uppy, uppy, Abram, no-longer-hungry, begs. Sweet boy.
        But when I pick him up he is not, actually, a boy but has become a human form
of metal. He is enchanted. Atomic. I must find a chalice. *Please,* I beg him. *Take this.*
        I offer cherry. I offer grape. I offer tropical fruit. Liquid. Chewable. Fastmelt.
With and without applesauce. *I can't,* he says. *I can't.* I say: *Please, please, please, please.*
        I say, *It would make me so happy.* You'll pay, mutter the audiences, for the sin of saying
smother, for saying these jewels of your womb are not the root of happiness

but are, rather, a toxic love-vapor, a poison, an addictive swill of life force. For saying
so, for saying these truths, how you're smothered and smithered by years
of unremitting love. *Please*, I say. *For me, for me, to make me happy…*
And he takes the purple fever-reducing pill, sweet boy full of trust, full of something
I need to stay alive, something I never knew to want before I could have wanted him,
and he puts it in his mouth. He winces. He chews. He swallows. He leans in
close and I smell his sweet grapey breath and he… pukes.
Now, he says, looking me right in my smithered, smothered eye, *are you happy?*

AFTER BABY AFTER BABY

When we made love you had
the dense body of a Doberman
and the square head of a Rottweiler.

With my eyes closed I saw:
a light green plate with seared scallops
and a perfect fillet of salmon on a cedar plank.

Now I am safe in the deep V of a weekday
wanting to tell you how the world
is full of street signs and strollers
and pregnant women in spandex.

The bed and desk both want me.
The windows, the view, the idea of Paris.

With my minutes, I chip away at the idiom,
an unmarked pebble in a fast current. Later,
on my way to the store, a boy with a basketball
yells, *You scared?* to someone else, and the things
on the list to buy come home with me.
And the baby. And your body.

SATURDAY, SUNDAY, MONDAY, TUESDAY

Saturday morning
two hawks flew over the soccer field and swooped in low
as Abram almost scored a goal. Moses, on the sideline, sat
on a stray ball reading a book, not looking up at the game
or the hawks or his brother who noticed. That night
at the Basic Trust Day Care Poker Tournament I got knocked
out with queen/nine against queen/jack by Dan Shiffman
who seemed almost sad to beat me. I sucked on ginger candies
and held new baby Phoebe Kate, born on the same due date
as the baby I miscarried. When she left I cried and had more candies.
In the end, Josh beat everyone and won a 40-inch flat-screen TV.

Sunday morning
I couldn't sleep so got up early, went to the Hell's Kitchen
flea market and bought a dining table and chairs from a man
named Toney. Bargained him down to $690 (including delivery)
because "the chairs need new upholstery." A 1950ish Danish
with expandable top and funny splayed feet—it reminds me
of my late Grandma Lotty, her sister Marguerite, and the heavy-laden
tables of childhood. I've no idea what it will look like
with my small family gathered round or if I'll overworry
the polished surface. We'll see—
it arrives on Tuesday.

This morning
I got a stack of papers from sophomore lit. The top two
had the author's name misspelled. I've not yet looked at
any others. I talked in class about how Art Spiegelman
chose realism over sentiment, how we conflate historical time
with personal time, how on 9/11 I took my nine-month old son

to his first day of day care and the city exploded, went up
in smoke, and no one but me cares that he spent hours there,
only nine months old, while we watched TV in our phone-jammed
airspace, breathed in fumes, tried to give blood, wondered was there
anywhere, anywhere we could or should

                                                    flee to?—

Josh called right after class and said he'd gotten "strong intent" from an agent
who's "all about the money."

Nothing disastrous happened this week. Not so far. Unless you count
what I saw next, between classes on my way to read student poems
at Empanada Mama's on 48th and 9th. A teenage boy lying on his side
in the middle of the street. The traffic stopped and a crowd watched
while six or seven other boys ran back and forth and stamped down
hard on his skull. I turn a gag into a kind of cough and dial 911.
We've already called the fucking police, says a woman as I retch
into an empty trash can. Finally three teenage girls surround the boy
and the other boys move off.

                                        Later,
on my way back to Fordham, I stop a cop and ask
about the boy. *EMTs got him*, says the officer.
They had no shame, no fear, even with all of us watching… I tell him.
They're kids, ma'am, he says. *You know what kids is like.*

                                        Tonight
in Writer's Workshop I & II I read two cantos from *Model Homes*
by Wayne Koestenbaum and then "A Poet's Life" by David Trinidad.
These poets hijack form and make it present, contemporary, immediate. Look how
Wayne puts a plumber and lovers, his mother, porn mags, fashion into terza rima
that lead us along, punch drunk, addicted to real life. And oh how David's crown

of sonnets breaks our hearts! The students stare blankly; one:
        These are sonnets?
and someone's cell phone rings with the sound of a human voice pleading:
Pick up! Pick up! Pick up!

                                        After an hour
we head upstairs to hear Linda Gregg, Saskia Hamilton, and Tess Gallagher.
Linda says, *I had a husband once named John and we did mushrooms*
and John said, "We're lost but hey don't worry because when it gets dark I can read
the stars" and I said "I don't know what you're talking about. We're not lost.
We're right here." And my students, aghast at who knows what,
start passing notes and rustling papers. Tess talks about her cancer
and the ghosts within and Saskia reads poems thick with grief,
some in a cracked guttural tongue I think is Danish.

                                        When I get home
and try to describe the boy in the street Josh says, *More people died*
in Iraq this month than any other and I remind him that tomorrow morning,
before the new table is due to be delivered, we're going to Saint Vincent's
Hospital where Dr. Margano will put the KY-covered wand inside me
and tell us if these past nine weeks have yielded a fetal heartbeat
which will change everything, nothing.

DON'T SAY ANYTHING BEAUTIFUL KISS ME

Anyway,
    if my lips were rose petals they'd taste too bitter.
If my cheeks were apples they'd crawl with apple worms.
If my eyes were stars they'd be dead by the time you saw them.
If I moved you like the moon I'd disappear once a month.
If my teeth were Chiclets you'd want to chew on them and spit them out.
If my hands were birds you couldn't hold them; they'd peck you bloody.
Is my skin alabaster? Then it's cold and hard and one day someone will skin me,
    make me into a cold hard box tinged with pink or yellow, to hold unguents, then
    how will you love me?
If my vagina is a cool, dark forest you'll certainly be lost, you have no sense of direction.
If my vagina is a cave—watch out! It's prone to seismic shifts and avalanche.
If my vagina is a river of honey: orange, lavender, fine herbs, hazelnut, all too sweet.
If my ears are shells I can't hear you, only the ocean anyway.
And if my voice is music, it is unintelligible.
Don't say anything.
I am not a flower, but a body with rules and predictable, cellular qualities.
My eyelashes and fingernails and skin and spit are organized by proteins
    designed to erode at a pre-encoded date and time, no matter what you do or do
    not do to me—
I am remarkably like an animal.
More like a heifer than a sunrise, I want to bite, stroke, swallow you so stop lying
    there trying to think of something to say and trying to understand me.
I am the body next to but unlike yours.
You already know me. You already know what I'm made of.

SUNDAY MORNING

Last night I woke up sweating and begged you
to open the open window and threw my damp
nightclothes to the floor none of which woke you.
Now the bedroom is crisp and I'm almost too big
to be on my back like this reading. Thinking you'll
touch me. Would you care to? Thirteen years later
a soft body under the sheets in a cold room
isn't a recipe for anything necessarily. The boys
are all set up with TV, my book's a decoy, and
a few weeks ago you said you liked
my hair. Can a woman this pregnant be shy?

Light shines in through the windows around
the taped-up shade samples. Maybe I should iChat you:
sex? That worked once. Or phone-to-phone
page you or text you: **my dragon tattoo
wont last thru another shower.** What if you
wanted to lick it? What if you wanted to bite
my inner thigh? What if you wanted to take the book
from my hands and rip it down the spine?

Your study is three rooms away but I know you can hear
the Spanish music pumping from the car stopped
at the light, eleven floors down. What if sound
condenses as it rises to meet us? What if you wanted
to bend me over the bed, belly be damned,
and that desire, three rooms away, was a sharpened
arrow by the time it reached me?

Our son is whistling Suzuki Violin Book Volume One
just outside the bedroom door, which is my punishment
for teaching him to whistle. I hear the toilet flush and wonder

if our younger one will wash with soap and water. What if
you saw me right now and said, *If you move I'll kill you,
you're so beautiful—?* What if my darkened nipples
intrigued you? I just read "touch the door like it's
someone's wife" in the book I'm reading,
which you didn't write. One of the samples snaps
against the window on its Scotch-taped hinge. You're
in the kitchen putting something ceramic on the stone-topped
counter. What if you wanted to drag me into our walk-in closet?
What if you wanted to press me up against the front door?
What if you wanted to disturb my sleep? *Why didn't you eat
your orange slices?* you ask the boys, while unpacking Friday's lunch.

Then all three handsets in the bedroom ring at once,
you come in to answer, see me reading, hold out the phone—
I'm sleeping, I say, hoping you get my meaning. You
don't. Instead return with the boys' leftover breakfast
and eat it lying next to me. I read you the poem about
touching the door. *Isn't it good?* I ask. *I've got a bad feeling
you're going to want one of the pots in the dishwasher
in the next twenty minutes but they're just not available,* you say.

I can almost see you through the open bathroom door,
through the polka-dotted shower curtain, but mostly
I see your bent elbow when you raise your hand to wash
your hair. When I touch myself the baby quite politely
goes to sleep. Then I'm a belly but no one inside me.
What if you didn't want me to put clothes on? What if
you wanted to sleep with my breast in your hand? What if
you liked poetry? What if you said, There's a closet
in the basement near the laundry room—meet me
there. *The best scene in the movie was him walking out
on the ice,* is what you do say, wrapped in a towel, looking
for the hairbrush. Mark Wahlberg playing Bobby Mercer

going to kick the shit out of a black gangster way out
on the thick-topped ice in Detroit, long coat open in the cold,
wooden cross around his neck bouncing against his thermal
chest. *You know*, you say, *Jeffrey McDaniel should NOT
talk shit about Joshua Beckman*, and I think: I like the way you
look, beefy and damp from your shower. You're definitely
my type—do you like that? Or would it be better to be
my one exception? Did you know there are men who like
a woman pregnant? I can feel their eyes on me—at the school,
the bus stop, the grocery—and men who shudder when I approach.
You're not quite either. What if you were? What if you wanted
to run your finger over the smooth almost imperceptible
stretch marks which have flattened out against my lower
abdomen or the funny ridge of pubis or the slope of my
lower back when I stand? When the baby comes we'll be married
ten, together thirteen years. What if that seemed like
a day? What if my naked body shocked you? What if yours
in the shower roused me? What if we sent the boys next door
to the neighbor?

What if you wanted to double click me more than your favorite,
latest download? What if you wanted to know me as much as
Baltar wants to know if he's a Cylon or Locke wants to know
what's in the hatch, except I mean *know* in the biblical sense. Or,
because of the baby you put in me, do you think you already do?
Do you think I'm all known up?

What if you wanted to bed me more than you'd like to stop
the war or see a good Democrat in office? And what if you
thought I was that unattainable? What if you couldn't find your
wallet but didn't care because I'd just walked into the room and you
thought I was sexier than Britta Phillips and you sang like Dean
Wareham and the crowd went crazy and the bootleggers shut up
their machines because no one could bear to share us, even recalling

our smoky glances makes them wild for what we have and what if the long poem is a kind of monogamy that you don't like either but count on. What if you wanted me the way you want coffee? What if you wanted to wake me up when I was sleeping? What if you knew what I was thinking?

MORE ACCIDENTS

it's 2007, in the back of the Buick.
the boy knows how he feels
and is not afraid to say it.

blood from his head, his knuckles, his knees, his wrist,
on my pants, my T-shirt, my hands.

                    I'm going to DIE! he screams
into the Buick's interior. our new baby in the car seat screaming.
purple-faced, wanting to be picked up. our biggest boy crying,
scared for or of his screaming brothers.

the Buick moving through suburban Denver
through the rain toward urgent care
and the double rainbow that is just then
gathering—

what was I thinking? *don't crash?*

husband at the wheel steering us, pushing the car
through space and time to urgent care the interior
titrated with the sound of screaming—molecules
or humidity of tears replacing or absorbing oxygen
until I'm breathing in the sound of their screaming,
the sound of M's wet face,
                the question mark of his face.

listen to my breathing, I say.

but A is fully engaged with the idea of dying.

why am I sure he is not dying? some children do—

me and the three boys in the back of the Buick and Josh
driving us through the August rain.

if we opened the window
would the sound fill the suburbs?
would the Buick empty out?
and if we could breathe deeply,
take in and in, deeply,
in all this crying—then what?

this is my family. this accident. these boys. this screaming.

the hard plastic edge of the car seat. the rhythmic crashing
of his short-haired boy-head against my collarbone.

&

later he will explain he turned around
to make sure his brother
was following. and when he turned back
couldn't right himself. and his wrist wasn't right.

and this is the accident. of being younger.
wanting to make sure. and this was there,
in the Buick, these boys, how they are tied
together in ways that do and do not include me.

the hopeful gaze.
the tether.
the broken.

M running to get us, tell us,
his brother and his not-right wrist.

&

later, A will say he was not scared.
he will laugh when I remind him he said he was going to die.

later, he will die, and I know this.

&

all the poems I've read, like music, have damaged me—

       deranger (accident), to bother (accident), unarrange (accident).
       vertical (accident). tower of (accident). tongues (accident) and
       (men jumping from—) postmodern (accident).
       past/future/present (accident).

—made me restless. are tough on marriage.

&

did you know there are perfect children
buried alive and frozen to death
in underground caverns all along
the Salta mountains?

perfect and perfectly preserved
by the morbid cold and dry, thin air.

mine were never perfect and therefore spared from sacrifice.

&

&

this is my family. mortals on our way to mortality
and around and in and out of accidents.

&

and this is what, just my museum? every country has one.
with rooms of hair and children's shoes and a woman holding
one child while the tsunami sweeps the other away and a whole city
going underwater and what people eat for breakfast and one place
left on earth without human beings the planet beset with plague and
a room of women giving birth to babies under anesthesia called
twilight restrained so later they will not appear unsightly—what
medicine was that? accident. and step this way are rooms and rooms
and within these other museums of explosions and planes and fish so
luminous we can't imagine and words—

&

planes have taken me all over the world
without incident. some brought me
into harm's way but no harm befell me

&

———where we enter and leave is irrelevant but means
everything. where/what/to whom we are born and if we ———

&

we're moving from room to room [they call these stanzas] seat of
muses, poems can't do justice just some engraved frescos in the hall
of wonders ——

&
&
&

: : : boxes, memory, polling booth, middle of the road, attempt,
thwarted attempt, for fuck's sake, slapstick, rented van, sandbag,
mass graves, levees, subway, high tide, world view, countdown,
medication, exterminator, John Berryman, Sylvia Plath, Allen
Ginsberg, Alice Notley, also, but in a different way: Spalding Gray
and Monica Lewinsky

cockpit, grassy knoll, bulletproof, wandering eye, gentile, fertility,
prose, soccer, poker, wayne, david, doug, arielle

&

&

"beginning, middle, end"

tell it again

&

to happen. to fall.

&

as a boat passes beneath a bridge
there is a specific height at which
(considering the tide and cargo)

it will not pass.
either above or below that line, accident.

story accident.

what happens accident.

&

neither the past either

&

or "happy accident"

what they're calling the female orgasm
which seems to be unrelated to fertility
and has no evolutionary purpose

&

fluke. serendipity.

these too are accidents.

&

one man made perfect pineapples out of butter.

along the fence tufts of wool caught in the starry barbs.

&

as if doing (something) were (simply) a matter of (choosing) what to
do.

&

it was 2003. M was three. A was 18 months.
there was no blighted ovum or new baby yet.
just us walking home from day care. I'm carrying
A and M walking by my side. we were coming out
of a long dark season but weren't out yet and walking
home, each step heavy, I think it was April and there was
outdoor seating in front of Acqua on Amsterdam and adults
having drinks and early dinners and I stepped toward the street,
A on my left hip, M on my left side. M stepped out in front of me I
couldn't see and then. happen. fall. accidere. cadere. I can't. see can
see. and time is everything is falling and I see us from above or
the side and my god I am and I shift my hand over his head
my god I am going to fall and crush him, my other son
will break my fall and cement. is so. slowly. coming up.
and up and up we are not falling. you see the world
has turned is coming up to meet us and I am
trying to twist, fly, to stop, there is a child
my child or precious "stumbling block"
in my path and a child precious in my
arms and the sidewalk is coming
for him and I am trying to find
the sky and save us. twisting
and twisting and thinking
bird? covering his head
with my hand
just knuckles
between
skull and
cement
and

my many knees in the other boy's where is he even? what parts of him?
and we are down now a heap people trying to help us precious

screaming and I'm rolling off him and looking for blood and they are
screaming I think, they are breathing, and my neck feels backwards but
works and I'm trying to gather can't stand so just sit down and try to
bring them in, close, to bring the screaming in and in to me and A
screams hard into me but M pulls away and looks at me eye to eye,
angry, *why did you do that?* he asks me. why?

&

too many children and not even all I'll have born yet.

& & &

this was an accident of nature
this was an accident of being born into money
accident of trying but not getting hooked
accident of sex
accident of pleasure
accident of adolescence and one man in a trench coat masturbating
and waving at me and Joan in the park and we're laughing and
running away and nothing worse
accident of being followed but not accosted
accident of girlhood
accident of English
accident of my father with many faces
accident of a mother too much how she loves stories
accident of crowded subways of the city filled with people and stories
and words and words and words and words and words and words
and words and words and words and words
birds
joy
New York
flock of pigeons changing direction above Central Park
rhyme

chance meetings
dreams

&

I'll take you, my father said, 1968.

and he did. by taxi. my mother would never
have thought to—even at a time like this—there'd never been
a time—

&

accident of narrative which is to say marrying from which followed
fertility also monotheism in this case secular

&

                                        are
born from it

are it   I am

this that

            I am

&

and Dean Wareham singing even after the band
breaks up, is picking at my seams and I'm yelling at our sons
and disappointed again and writing the same poem

&

accident of one man but not another which is to say marriage

&

wifeliness and waves
birth I mean birthing

proximity, infestation, habitation, habituation, joy, terror, loneliness,
smallness, anger, injury, damage, lust, targets, language, fortune,
worth

the afternoon before the birth of our third baby you met Philip Roth
on a bench in Central Park and talked to him until Abram pitched a
fit. *isn't your family enough?* asked Roth.

&

points on a map
marks on a page
Jews from other countries

marriage. charity. hard candy.

an ark or kind of rain.

&

accident of waking
accident of sleep

of sunlight
the shutter button
sniper, miscreant

of safety and longing
of danger and grief

&

       it was there in the Buick, on the question mark of his face:

                  why?

&

I sent three boats goes the joke about the great believer
who died in a flood and was angry at God.

Philip Roth telling you to be happy with what you have.

&

other punchlines

&

short stories like:

my father was indispensable.
my mother a great beauty.

and out of this:

&

bodies, features, health, disease, time distance chance

this is not the accident.
this is not the accident.
I can't imagine

what is not the accident.

except what I see
what part   I know
part   part
is the accident

when I say there is no accident
it is
the accident

of telling and not telling of selecting and forgetting

the juncture and/or juxtoposition where things
come together and

don't

swerve, synapse, mis/under/standings

[death is not the accident]
life is

POEM

The other day Matt Rohrer said,
the next time you feel yourself going dark
in a poem, just don't, and see what happens.

That was when Matt, Deborah Landau,
Catherine Barnett, and I were chatting,
on our way to somewhere and something else.

In her office, a few minutes earlier, Deborah
had asked, are you happy? And I said, um, yes,
actually, and Deborah: well, *I'm* not—

all I do is work and work. And the phone
rang every thirty seconds and between
calls Deborah said, I asked Catherine

if she was happy and Catherine said, life
isn't about happiness it's about helping
other people. I shrugged, not knowing how

to respond to such a fine idea.
So, what makes *you* happy?
Deborah asked, in an accusatory way,

and I said, I guess, the baby, really,
because he makes me stop
working? And Deborah looked sad

and just then her husband called
and Deborah said, Mark, I've got
Rachel Zucker here, *she's* happy,

I'll have to call you back. And then
we left her office and went downstairs
to the salon where a few weeks before

we'd read poems for the *Not for Mothers Only*
anthology and I especially liked Julie Carr's
poem about crying while driving while listening to

the radio report news of the war while her kids
fought in the back seat while she remembered
her mother crying while driving, listening to

news about the war. There were a lot of poems
that night about crying, about the war, about
fighting, about rage, anger, and work. Afterward

Katy Lederer came up to me and said,
"I don't believe in happiness"—you're such a bitch
for using that line, now no one else can.

Deborah and I walked through that now-sedated space
which felt smaller and shabby without Anne Waldman
and all those women and poems and suddenly

there was Catherine in a splash of sunlight
at the foot of a flight of stairs talking to Matt Rohrer
on his way to a room or rooms I've never seen.

And that's when Deborah told Matt that I was
happy and that Catherine thought life wasn't about
happiness and Deborah laughed a little and flipped

her hair (she is quite glamorous) and said, but Matt,
are *you* happy? Well, Matt said he had a bit of a cold
but otherwise was and that's when he said,

next time you feel yourself going dark in a poem,
just don't, and see what happens. And then,
because it was Julian's sixth birthday, Deborah went

to bring him cupcakes at school and Catherine and I
went to talk to graduate students who teach poetry
to children in hospitals and shelters and other

unhappy places and Matt went up the stairs to the room
or rooms I've never seen. That was last week and now
I'm here, in bed, turning toward something I haven't felt

for a long while. A few minutes ago I held our baby up
to the bright window and sang the song I always sing
before he takes his nap. He whined and struggled

the way toddlers do, wanting to move on to something
else, something next, and his infancy is almost over.
He is crying himself to sleep now and I will not say

how full of sorrow I feel, but will turn instead
to that day, only a week ago, when I was
the happiest poet in the room, including Matt Rohrer.

THE DEATH OF EVERYTHING EVEN NEW YORK CITY

what do I need with the ocean?
and what do I need with the sky?
Dean Wareham

Even if there are Starlings, well, fuck that.
And Blackbird? sorry. Mockingbird? nope. Robin,
Bluebird, Warbler, Mourning Dove—you're
kidding, right? Even the Coot, Vulture, Cowbird,
House Finch—the whole bird world is used up.

Even babies and lovers and language—might as well forget
flowers. The most contaminated flower in the world is too
beautiful, the worst marriage too romantic, the most malicious
baby too acutely precious and untrustworthy.

Today the government told us not to drink the water, not
to breathe the air, so when I do drink and breathe I've no one
to blame, and to write instead of the early morning playground,
the glorious breeze, feathered vertebrae, isn't credible
and that's a shame, because Starlings, charming name notwithstanding,
are a nuisance—noisy, nasty to other birds—a nice metaphor
for our sons, the way they *%&)@(&#!

but we're both terminally sick of "the way a…"
and whatever comes afterward.

Today I say shut down the Holland, Lincoln, and Midtown tunnels! I say
lock down the bridges and roads and waterways against the way anything
is like anything else. Say *No!* to fish named after colors, birds named
after mammals, flowers named after men. Even the names of diseases
are too clever, keen, apropos, disconcertingly lyrical. Eradicate adjectives
and all words beginning with A: anemia, areola, arroyo—they are all too
elegiac—and continue thus through the many alphabets that are passé.

The *New York Times* reports that since 1886 more than 200 species of birds
have been spotted in Central Park. The Great Blue Heron and Mute Swan
are year-round inhabitants. The Chimney Swift flies over daily in summer.

So what?

It's too late to describe the world.

Poor Bobolink. Bobwhite. Buzzard. Chickadee. Falcon.
Kingfisher. Solitaire. Sparrow. Thrush. We are all fed up with you.
Bloated. Stuffed. Sated and dissatisfied.

Once I said something to you so sincere it was pure, whole, heartfelt.
It was spontaneous and there was no crisis of language, no semiotic
hassle. Anomia was the name of a stubborn child and malignancy
didn't have a nice ring to it because it wasn't invented
and used online and in print 500 million times.

But that was just a dream. I won't write about dreams.

I swear: one day, perhaps not in our lifetime, we'll finally see
the death of everything and then, oh then, I'll be able to say once
a priori, before tropes and isotopes, the pastiche and list poem,
the rant and dirge, appropriation of French words into English,
to you, my husband, that in this toxic urban aviary especially
because of the contamination, because finally, when the death of
everything and the only bird left is the Cormorant and then that's
gone and Central Park is no longer a simile for the country because
there is no country is no farmland no park to offset the streets nor

streets the blocks and blocks of buildings, skyscrapers, low-rises,
air rights, underground water mains because there is no water no air
no micron of habitable atmosphere and then when the death of everything
and language is pure and there is not a single living man or woman to say
anything not even "primordial soup" or "big bang" I'll say,
I love you and it means something and you'll know it always did.

ACKNOWLEDGMENTS AND NOTES

Grateful acknowledgment is made to:

the editors—Deborah Ager, Joshua Beckman and Matthew Zapruder, Julie Carr, Wolfgang Görtschacher, Arielle Greenberg, Katy Lederer, Elizabeth Scanlon, Robin Beth Schaer, Jill Stengel, Michael Theune, David Trinidad, Nick Twemlow, and Sarah Vap—of the following publications where poems from this book first appeared: *32 poems*; *State of the Union: 50 Political Poems* (Wave Books, 2008), *English Language Notes*, *Poetry Salzburg Review*, *Black Clock*, *Explosive Magazine*, *The American Poetry Review*, poets.org, *MEM*, *Structure and Surprise* (Teachers & Writers Collaborative, 2007), *Columbia Poetry Review*, *The Canary*, *42opus*;

the childminders—Barbara Zucker, Ben Zucker, Diane Wolkstein, Lindsey Wallace, and Basic Trust Day Care—who make poetry possible;

the mothers of the furrow—Erin Murray Marra, Joan Platt, Dana DiPrima, Arielle Greenberg, and Stacy Nolan—who hear me call;

and Matthew Zapruder, who wanted this book.

The title of the book refers to a proposal by Paul Virilio for a new museum that would expose and exhibit "all accidents, from the most commonplace to the most tragic, from natural catastrophes to industrial and scientific disasters, including also the kind that is too often neglected, the happy accident, the stroke of luck, the coup de foudre or even the coup de grâce!"

The language in part 2 of "To Save America" comes from the exhibition House of Oracles: A Huang Yong Ping Retrospective, which I saw at the Walker Art Center in Minneapolis in 2005.

"The lightning, which doth cease to be / Ere one can say 'It lightens'" is from *Romeo and Juliet* by William Shakespeare.

"Haply I think on thee" is from Sonnet XXIX by William Shakespeare.

"But why compare? / I'm 'Wife'! Stop there!" is from poem 199 by Emily Dickinson.

"Touch the door like it's someone's wife" is from *In No One's Land* by Paige Ackerson-Kiely (Ahsahta Press, 2007).